Thor Welhaven

& Lourdes Welhaven

DREAM KITCHEN
Coloring Book

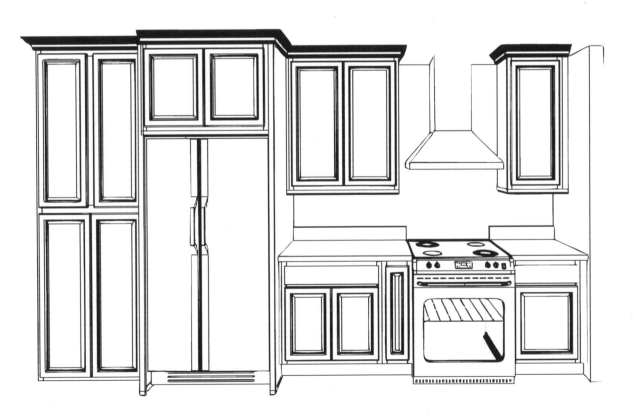

ISBN-13: 978-1535044424

ISBN-10: 153504442X

Cover and page design by Welhaven and Associates. For more information go to www.welhavenandassociates.com.

For more information on this and other home remodeling titles go to www.topdrawer.cc.

This book is more than just another adult coloring book. Certainly, I hope that you enjoy the art therapy that this book, like other amazing adult coloring books, provides. But by going through this book, you'll both discover as well as document your preferences.

Sometimes we just don't know what we like "until we see it." With the "Dream Kitchen Coloring Book," you'll be able to play and experiment with different layouts and colors to narrow down what appeals to you most.

If you like to color and that's all you're interested in, don't worry. This book has been constructed with the colorist in mind. For example, each sheet is one-sided. In this way, you don't have to worry about markers bleeding through a design on the reverse side of the sheet. There are also plenty of designs, 50 to be exact, each with differing levels of detail to keep things interesting.

But the book has also been created for those who love planning and dreaming about kitchens. There's a space below each design to document your color and texture preferences for the floor, ceiling, countertops, backsplashes, upper cabinets, lower cabinets, appliances and walls. By experimenting throughout the book, you'll begin to notice what works for you and what doesn't.

You'll find it interesting to note that the designs included are based on actual professional elevations that my company, Top Drawer Cabinetry & Carpentry, LLC, created in the course of our normal business operations. I chose certain layouts that include unique elements. You should consider whether or not you like them for your own kitchen. There are no right or wrong answers. Instead, use this coloring book as a workbook to get clear on your personal needs and preferences.

Thank you for purchasing Dream Kitchen Coloring Book. I hope it brings you many hours of coloring enjoyment and helps you to plan for a successful and beautiful kitchen remodeling project.

Thor Welhaven

TOP DRAWER
CABINETRY & CARPENTRY, LLC

IRC 16611 • SLC 28534 • MCAR6034 • FP 19986

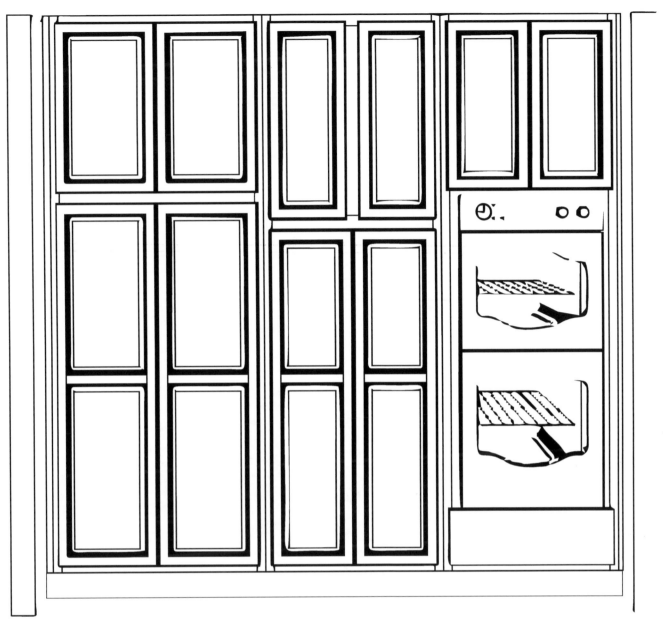

Floor _____

Ceiling _____

Countertop _____

Backsplash _____

Upper Cabinets _____

Lower Cabinets _____

Appliances _____

Walls _____

Design Question: Does a double oven make sense for you?

_____

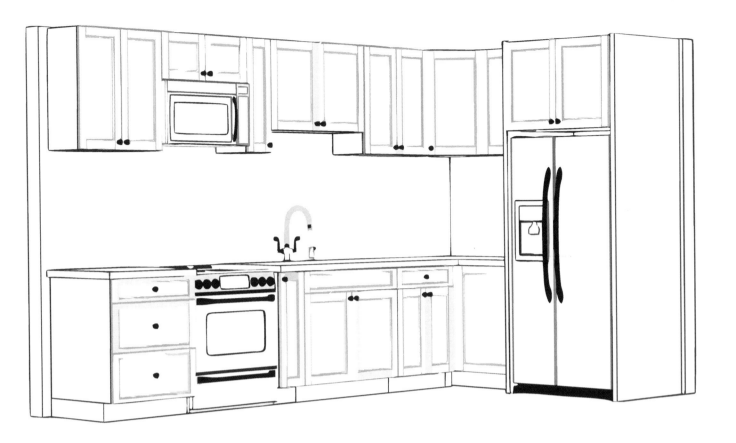

Floor _____

Ceiling _____

Countertop _____

Backsplash _____

Upper Cabinets _____

Lower Cabinets _____

Appliances _____

Walls _____

Design Question: Do you like a prep sink next to the stove?

_____

Floor _____

Ceiling _____

Countertop _____

Backsplash _____

Upper Cabinets _____

Lower Cabinets _____

Appliances _____

Walls _____

Design Question: Drawer/door combo or a full door cabinet?

_____

Floor _____

Ceiling _____

Countertop _____

Backsplash _____

Upper Cabinets _____

Lower Cabinets _____

Appliances _____

Walls _____

Design Question: Do you like the raised overhanging counter?

_____

Floor _____

Ceiling _____

Countertop _____

Backsplash _____

Upper Cabinets _____

Lower Cabinets _____

Appliances _____

Walls _____

Design Question: Do you like the tray cabinet next to the range?

_____

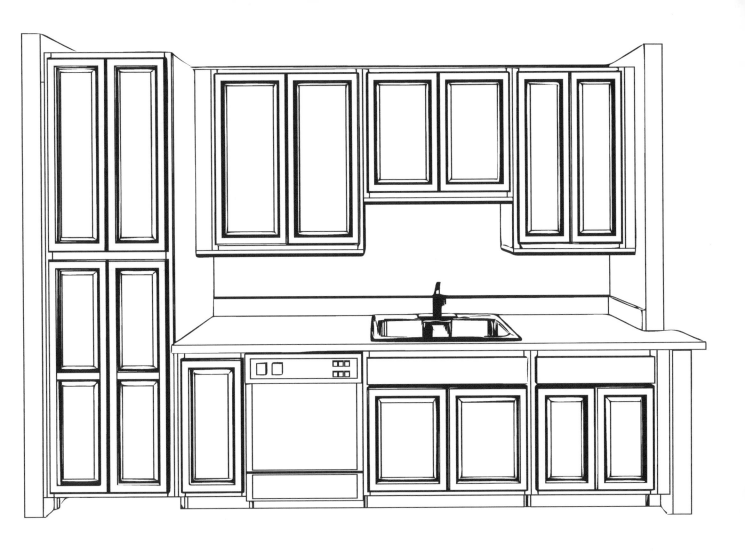

Floor _____

Ceiling _____

Countertop _____

Backsplash _____

Upper Cabinets _____

Lower Cabinets _____

Appliances _____

Walls _____

Design Question: Dishwasher to the left or right of the sink?

_____

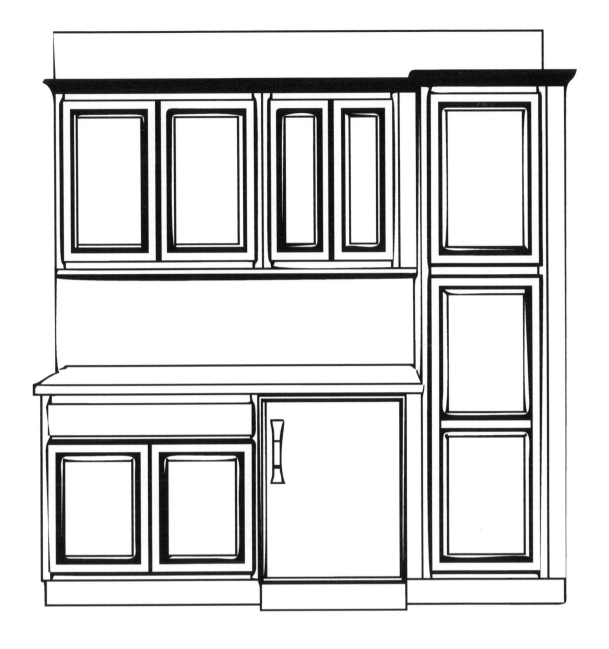

Floor _____

Ceiling _____

Countertop _____

Backsplash _____

Upper Cabinets _____

Lower Cabinets _____

Appliances _____

Walls _____

Design Question: Do you need under-cabinet refrigeration?

_____

Floor _____

Ceiling _____

Countertop _____

Backsplash _____

Upper Cabinets _____

Lower Cabinets _____

Appliances _____

Walls _____

Design Question: Do you like the wine rack?

_____

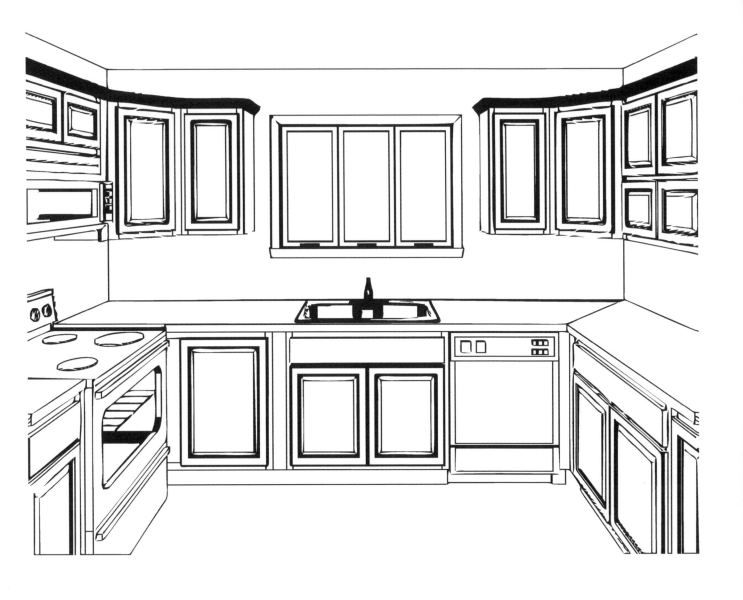

Floor _____

Ceiling _____

Countertop _____

Backsplash _____

Upper Cabinets _____

Lower Cabinets _____

Appliances _____

Walls _____

Design Question: Do you like the sink centered under the window?

_____

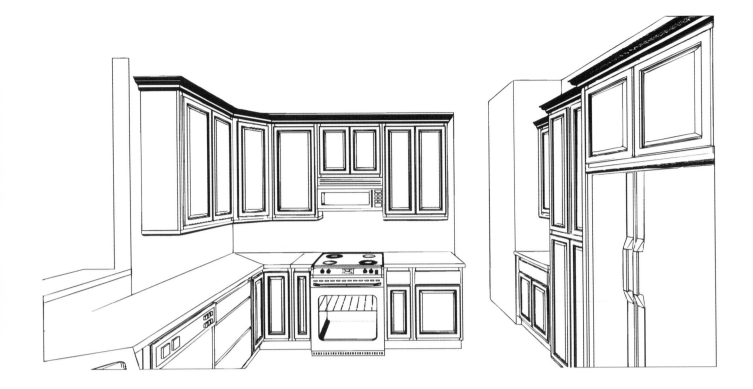

Floor _____

Ceiling _____

Countertop _____

Backsplash _____

Upper Cabinets _____

Lower Cabinets _____

Appliances _____

Walls _____

Design Question: Do you like the microwave over the range?

_____

Floor _____

Ceiling _____

Countertop _____

Backsplash _____

Upper Cabinets _____

Lower Cabinets _____

Appliances _____

Walls _____

Design Question: Do you like a cabinet over the refrigerator?

_____

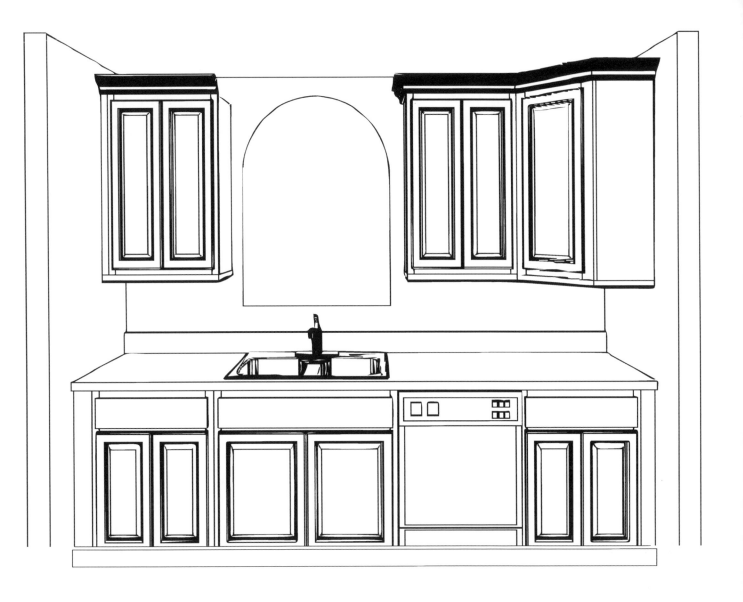

Floor _____

Ceiling _____

Countertop _____

Backsplash _____

Upper Cabinets _____

Lower Cabinets _____

Appliances _____

Walls _____

Design Question: Do you like the arched pass-thru?

_____

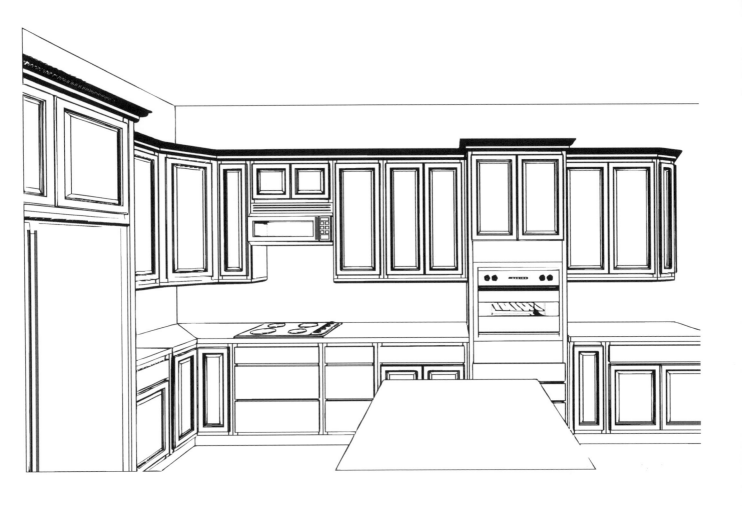

Floor _____

Ceiling _____

Countertop _____

Backsplash _____

Upper Cabinets _____

Lower Cabinets _____

Appliances _____

Walls _____

Design Question: Do like a built-in oven?

_____

Floor _____

Ceiling _____

Countertop _____

Backsplash _____

Upper Cabinets _____

Lower Cabinets _____

Appliances _____

Walls _____

Design Question: Do you like a smaller island?

_____

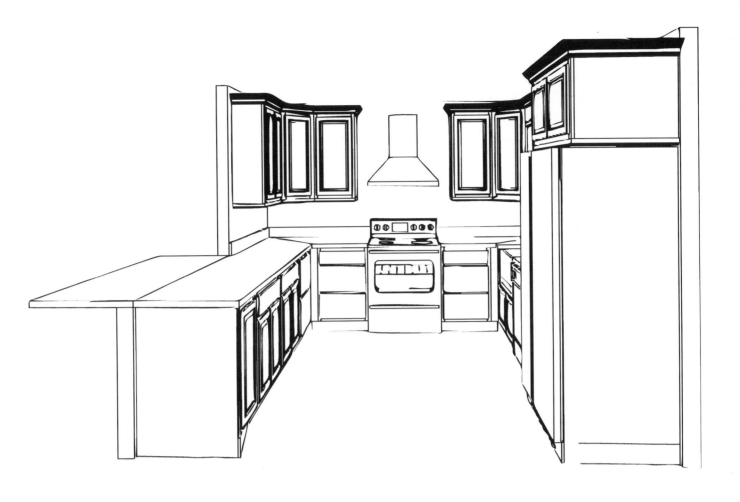

Floor _____

Ceiling _____

Countertop _____

Backsplash _____

Upper Cabinets _____

Lower Cabinets _____

Appliances _____

Walls _____

Design Question: Do you like an eat-in kitchen countertop?

_____

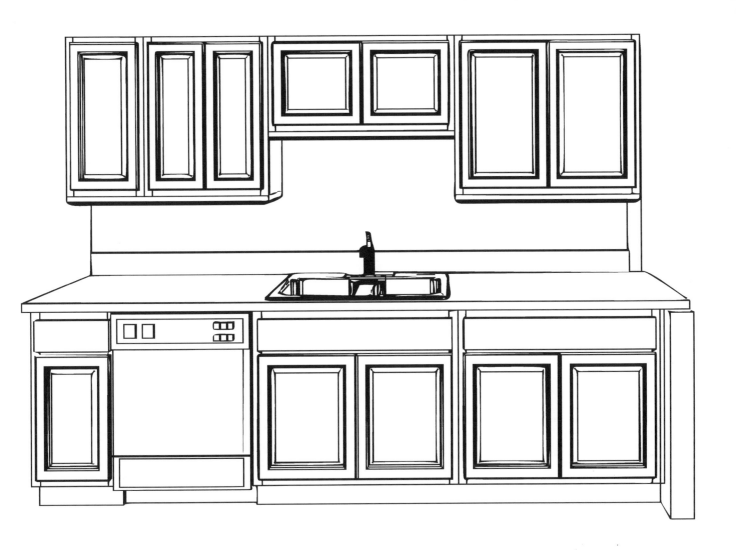

Floor _____

Ceiling _____

Countertop _____

Backsplash _____

Upper Cabinets _____

Lower Cabinets _____

Appliances _____

Walls _____

Design Question: Do you like cabinets over the sink?

_____

Floor _____

Ceiling _____

Countertop _____

Backsplash _____

Upper Cabinets _____

Lower Cabinets _____

Appliances _____

Walls _____

Design Question: Do you like a built-in tv in the kitchen?

_____

Floor _____

Ceiling _____

Countertop _____

Backsplash _____

Upper Cabinets _____

Lower Cabinets _____

Appliances _____

Walls _____

Design Question: Do you like a sink in a kitchen island?

_____

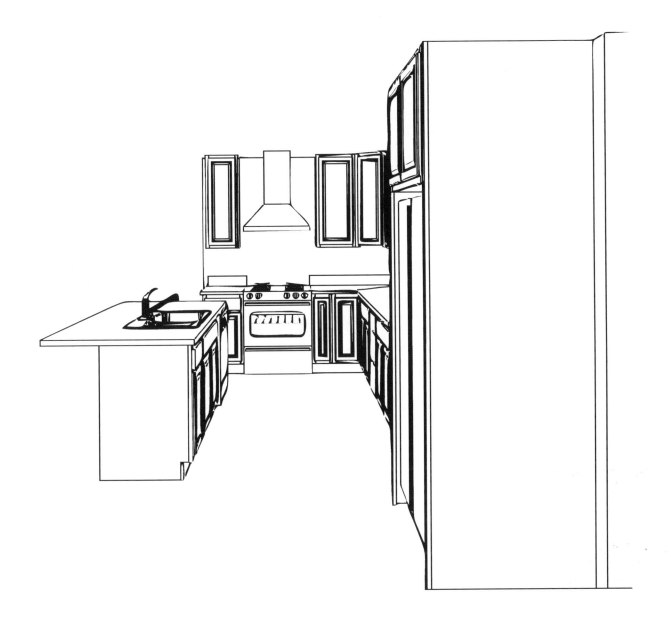

Floor _____

Ceiling _____

Countertop _____

Backsplash _____

Upper Cabinets _____

Lower Cabinets _____

Appliances _____

Walls _____

Design Question: What kind of hood do you like over the range?

_____

Floor _____

Ceiling _____

Countertop _____

Backsplash _____

Upper Cabinets _____

Lower Cabinets _____

Appliances _____

Walls _____

Design Question: Do you like an eat-in island?

_____

Floor _____

Ceiling _____

Countertop _____

Backsplash _____

Upper Cabinets _____

Lower Cabinets _____

Appliances _____

Walls _____

Design Question: Do you want a "lazy susan" in your kitchen?

_____

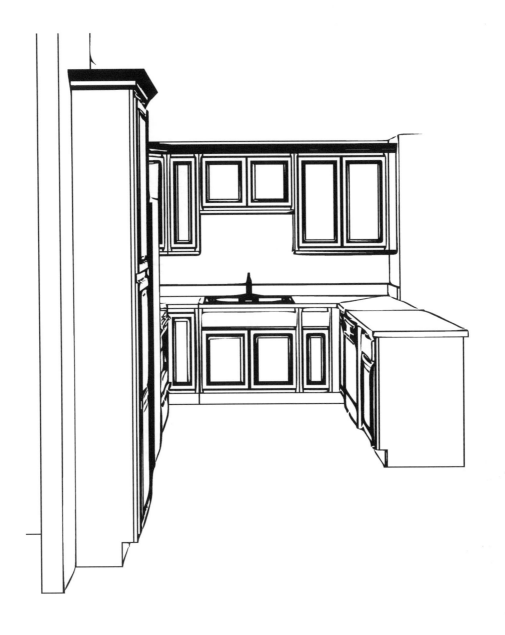

Floor _____

Ceiling _____

Countertop _____

Backsplash _____

Upper Cabinets _____

Lower Cabinets _____

Appliances _____

Walls _____

Design Question: Do you like crown-molding in your kitchen?

_____

Floor _____

Ceiling _____

Countertop _____

Backsplash _____

Upper Cabinets _____

Lower Cabinets _____

Appliances _____

Walls _____

Design Question: Does a bank of drawers make sense for you?

_____

Floor _____

Ceiling _____

Countertop _____

Backsplash _____

Upper Cabinets _____

Lower Cabinets _____

Appliances _____

Walls _____

Design Question: How tall do you want your backsplash to be?

_____

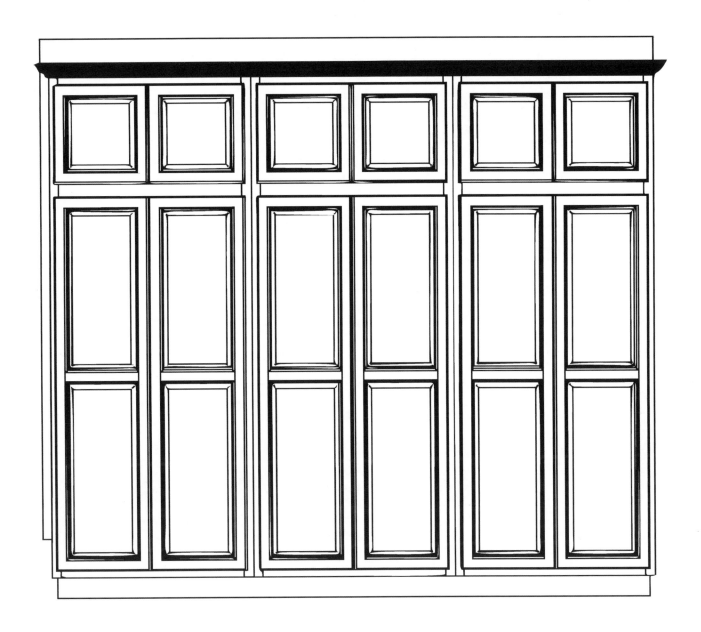

Floor _____

Ceiling _____

Countertop _____

Backsplash _____

Upper Cabinets _____

Lower Cabinets _____

Appliances _____

Walls _____

Design Question: Do you have room for pantry cabinets?

_____

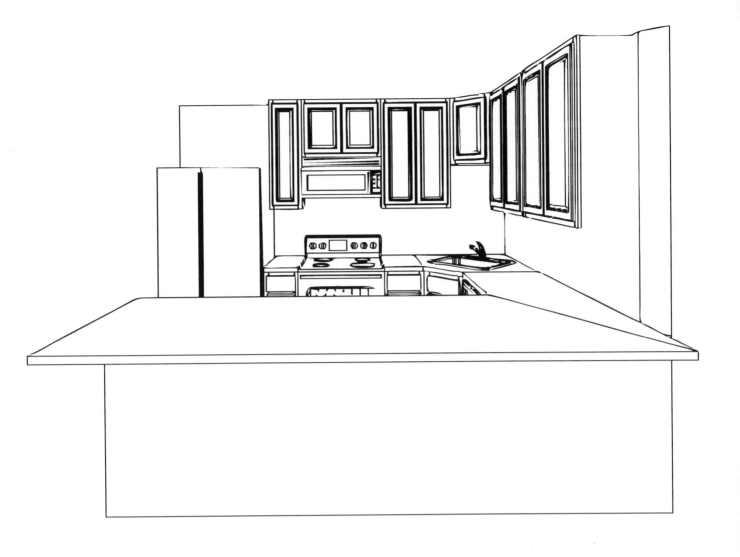

Floor _____

Ceiling _____

Countertop _____

Backsplash _____

Upper Cabinets_____

Lower Cabinets _____

Appliances _____

Walls _____

Design Question: Do you like having no cabinet over the fridge?

_____

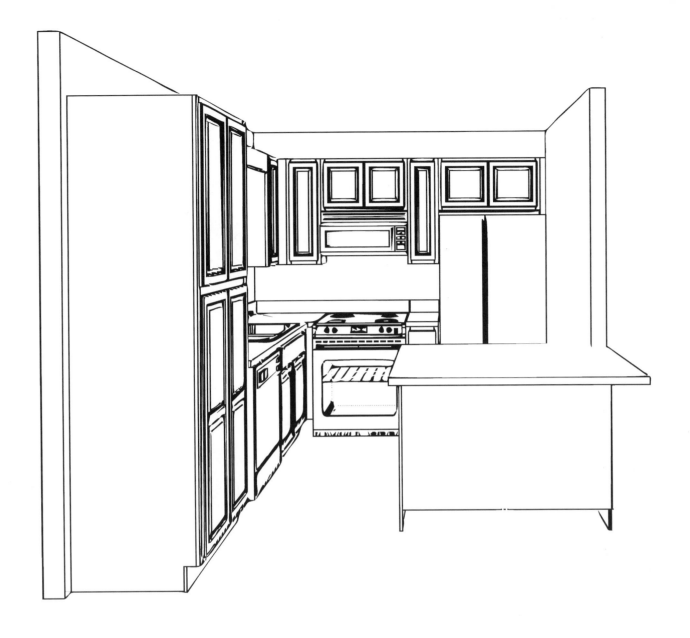

Floor _____

Ceiling _____

Countertop _____

Backsplash _____

Upper Cabinets _____

Lower Cabinets _____

Appliances _____

Walls _____

Design Question: Do you like having no crown-molding?

_____

Floor _____

Ceiling _____

Countertop _____

Backsplash _____

Upper Cabinets _____

Lower Cabinets _____

Appliances _____

Walls _____

Design Question: Do you like a valence over the sink?

_____

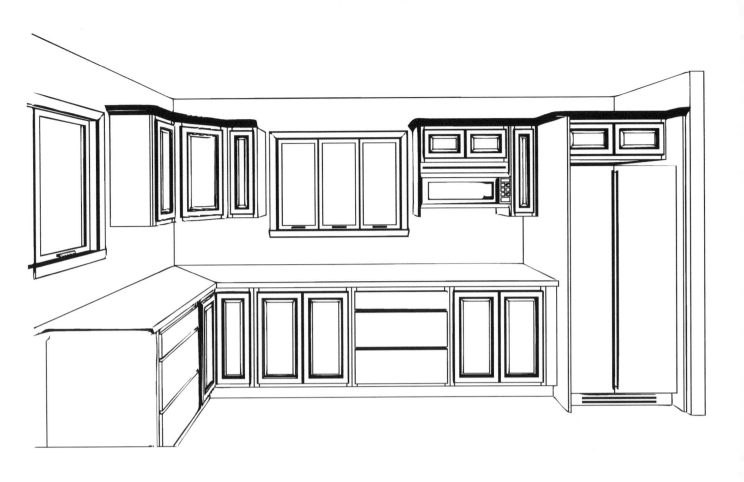

Floor _____

Ceiling _____

Countertop _____

Backsplash _____

Upper Cabinets _____

Lower Cabinets _____

Appliances _____

Walls _____

Design Question: Do you like a built-in look for a fridge?

_____

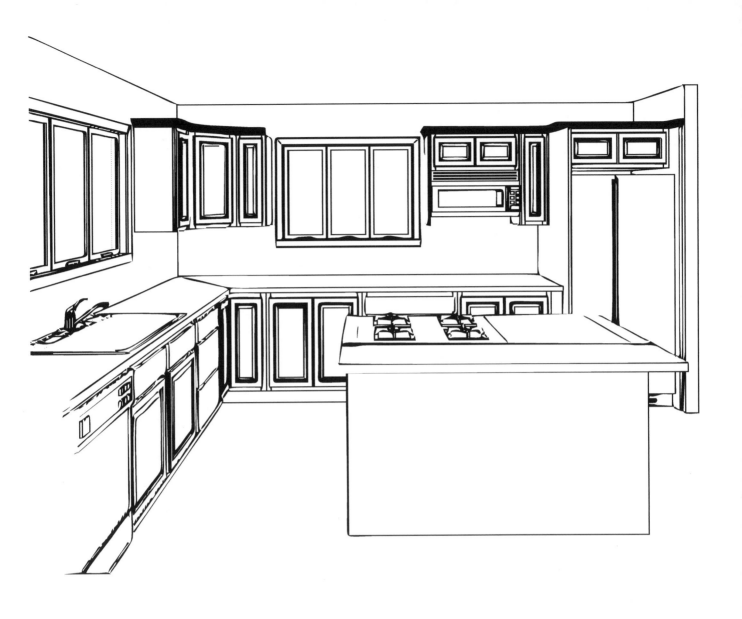

Floor _____

Ceiling _____

Countertop _____

Backsplash _____

Upper Cabinets _____

Lower Cabinets _____

Appliances _____

Walls _____

Design Question: Do you like a cooktop?

_____

Floor _____

Ceiling _____

Countertop _____

Backsplash _____

Upper Cabinets _____

Lower Cabinets _____

Appliances _____

Walls _____

Design Question: Do you like a prep-sink in the kitchen island?

_____

Floor _____

Ceiling _____

Countertop _____

Backsplash _____

Upper Cabinets _____

Lower Cabinets _____

Appliances _____

Walls _____

Design Question: Trash bin cabinet next to the dishwasher?

_____

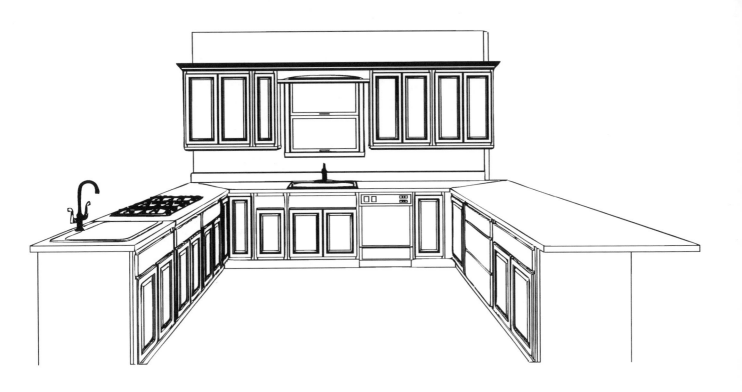

Floor _____

Ceiling _____

Countertop _____

Backsplash _____

Upper Cabinets _____

Lower Cabinets _____

Appliances _____

Walls _____

Design Question: Do you like a long countertop run?

_____

Floor _____

Ceiling _____

Countertop _____

Backsplash _____

Upper Cabinets _____

Lower Cabinets _____

Appliances _____

Walls _____

Design Question: Do you like double ovens next to a wall?

_____

Floor _____

Ceiling _____

Countertop _____

Backsplash _____

Upper Cabinets _____

Lower Cabinets _____

Appliances _____

Walls _____

Design Question: Do you want a flip-tray for your sink?

_____

Floor _____

Ceiling _____

Countertop _____

Backsplash _____

Upper Cabinets _____

Lower Cabinets _____

Appliances _____

Walls _____

Design Question: Do you like a range with the controls in the back?

_____

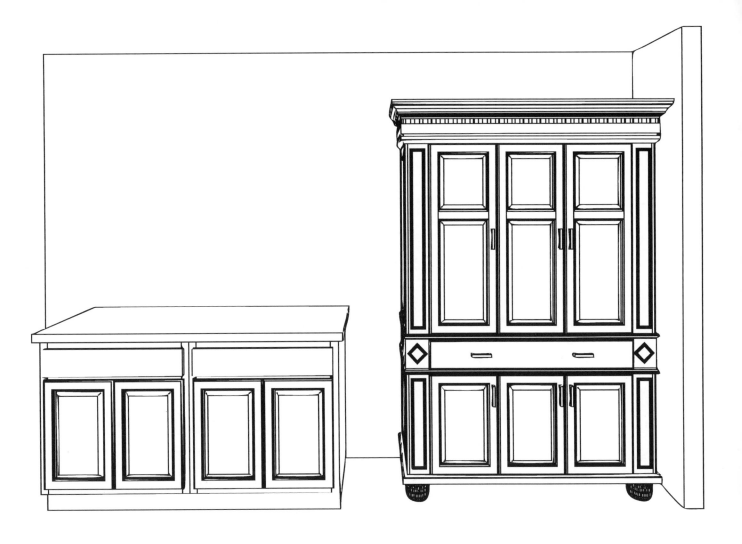

Floor _____

Ceiling _____

Countertop _____

Backsplash _____

Upper Cabinets _____

Lower Cabinets _____

Appliances _____

Walls _____

Design Question: Do you like a piece of furniture in your kitchen?

_____

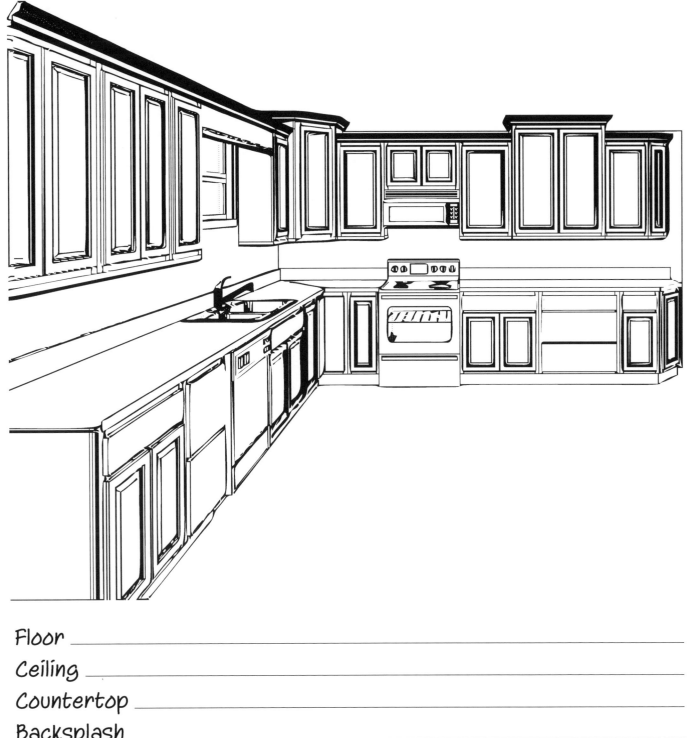

Floor _____

Ceiling _____

Countertop _____

Backsplash _____

Upper Cabinets _____

Lower Cabinets _____

Appliances _____

Walls _____

Design Question: Do you like the taller cabinets as accent pieces?

_____

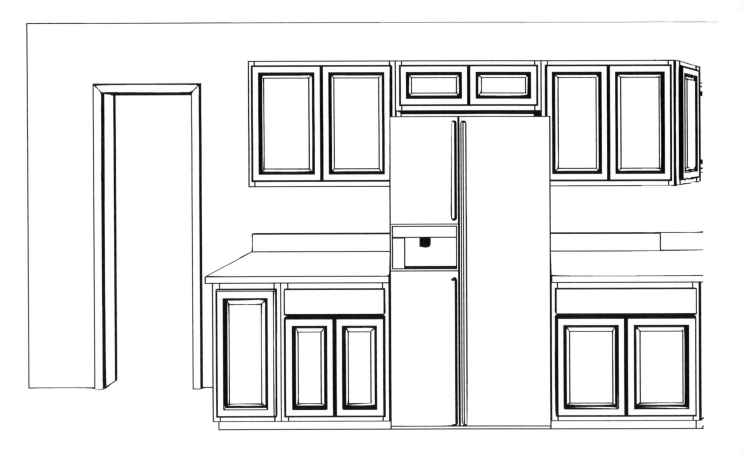

Floor _____

Ceiling _____

Countertop _____

Backsplash _____

Upper Cabinets _____

Lower Cabinets _____

Appliances _____

Walls _____

Design Question: Do you have a doorway to consider?

_____

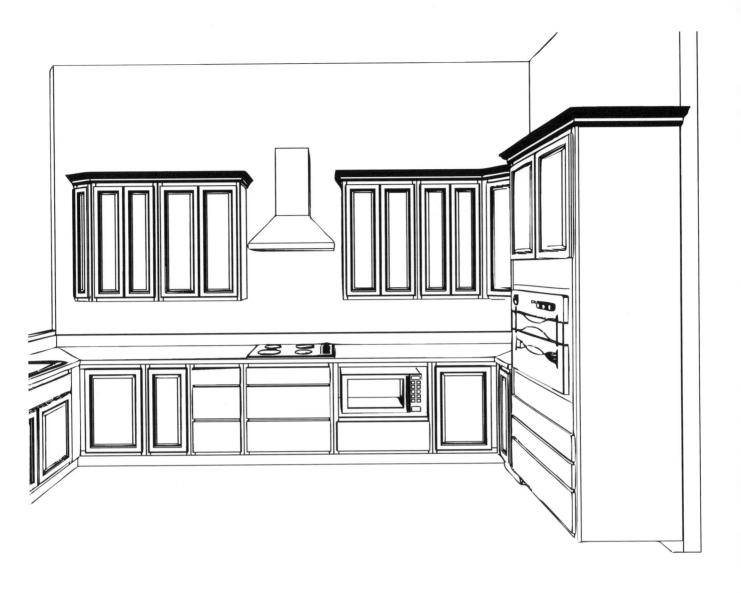

Floor _____

Ceiling _____

Countertop _____

Backsplash _____

Upper Cabinets _____

Lower Cabinets _____

Appliances _____

Walls _____

Design Question: Do you like an under-cabinet microwave?

_____

Floor _____

Ceiling _____

Countertop _____

Backsplash _____

Upper Cabinets _____

Lower Cabinets _____

Appliances _____

Walls _____

Design Question: Do you need specialty cabinets for tablecloths?

_____

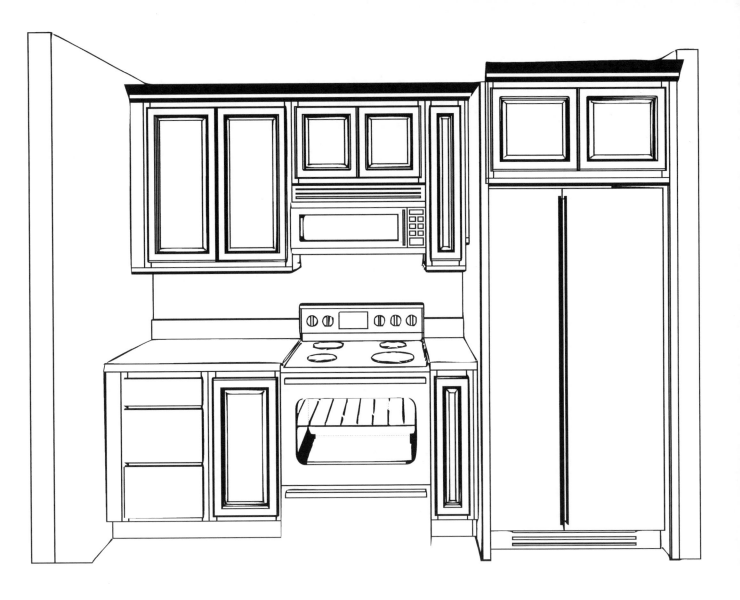

Floor _____

Ceiling _____

Countertop _____

Backsplash _____

Upper Cabinets _____

Lower Cabinets _____

Appliances _____

Walls _____

Design Question: How much counterspace is enough?

_____

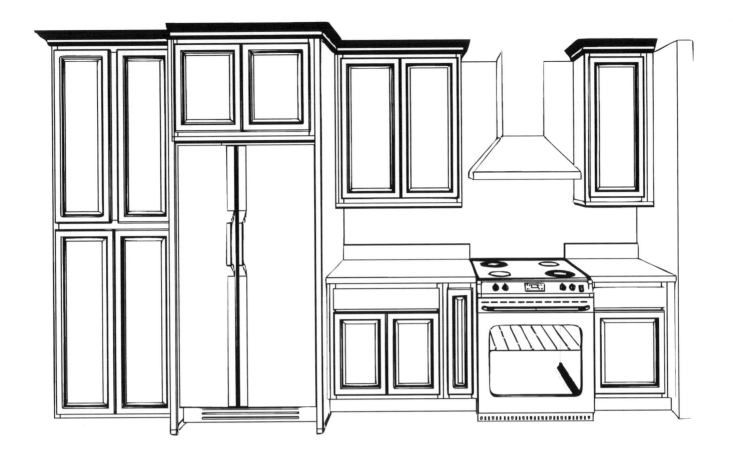

Floor _____

Ceiling _____

Countertop _____

Backsplash _____

Upper Cabinets _____

Lower Cabinets _____

Appliances _____

Walls _____

Design Question: Do you like tall cabinets next to the fridge?

_____

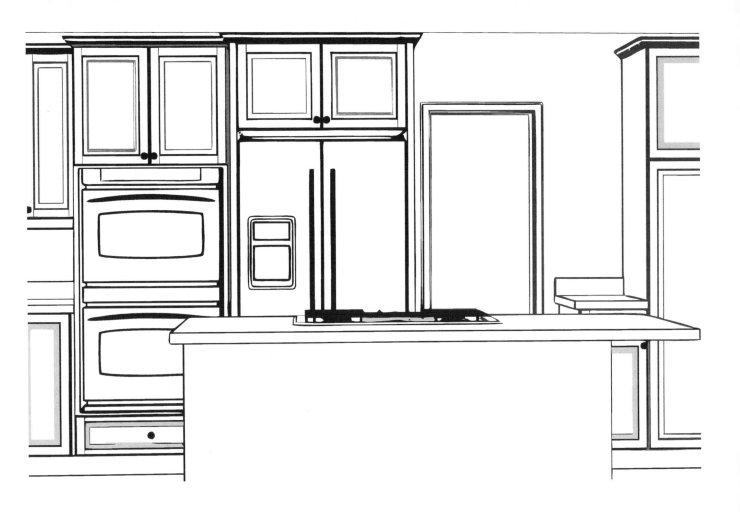

Floor _____

Ceiling _____

Countertop _____

Backsplash _____

Upper Cabinets _____

Lower Cabinets _____

Appliances _____

Walls _____

Design Question: Do you want ovens next to the fridge?

_____

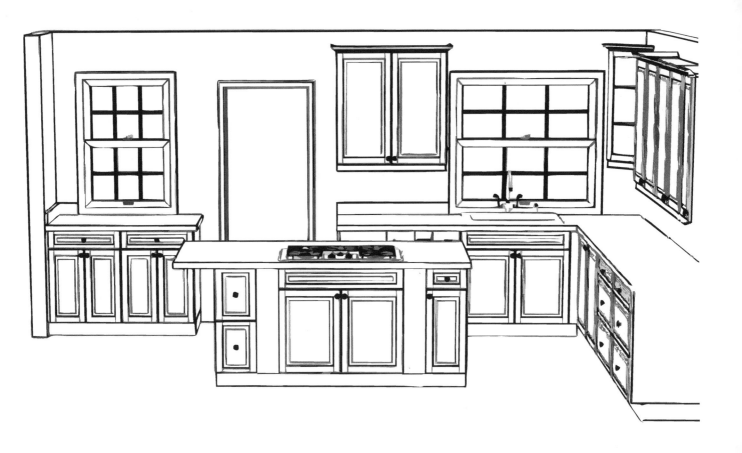

Floor _____

Ceiling _____

Countertop _____

Backsplash _____

Upper Cabinets _____

Lower Cabinets _____

Appliances _____

Walls _____

Design Question: Do you like a cabinet between a window and door?

_____

Floor _____

Ceiling _____

Countertop _____

Backsplash _____

Upper Cabinets _____

Lower Cabinets _____

Appliances _____

Walls _____

Design Question: Do you like Shaker-Style cabinet doors?

_____

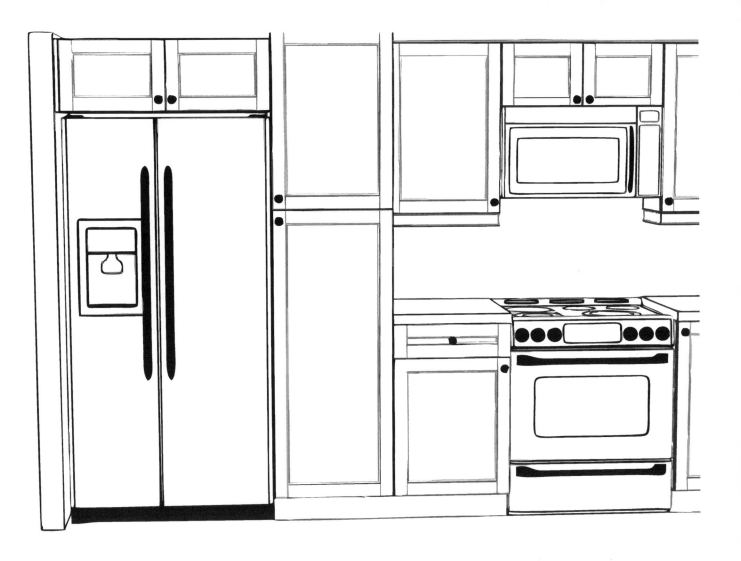

Floor _____

Ceiling _____

Countertop _____

Backsplash _____

Upper Cabinets _____

Lower Cabinets _____

Appliances _____

Walls _____

Design Question: What do you want your knobs to look like?

_____

Floor _____

Ceiling _____

Countertop _____

Backsplash _____

Upper Cabinets _____

Lower Cabinets _____

Appliances _____

Walls _____

Design Question: Do you have any sliding-glass doors to consider?

_____

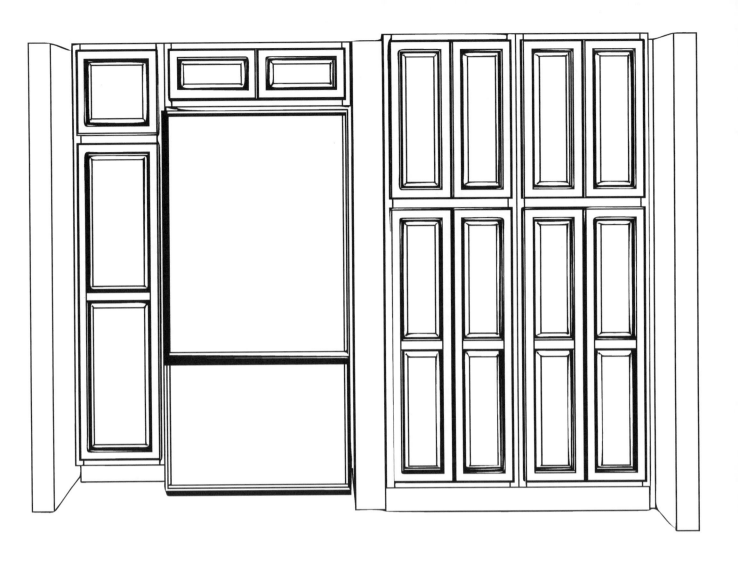

Floor _____

Ceiling _____

Countertop _____

Backsplash _____

Upper Cabinets _____

Lower Cabinets _____

Appliances _____

Walls _____

Design Question: More storage or more counter space?

_____

Floor _____

Ceiling _____

Countertop _____

Backsplash _____

Upper Cabinets _____

Lower Cabinets _____

Appliances _____

Walls _____

Design Question: Do you need a bar area?

_____

I hope you have enjoyed using "Dream Kitchen Coloring Book."

Please consider leaving a review of this book on Amazon.
Reviews make it possible for authors and creators to get their works discovered
by other people who might enjoy them also.

Meanwhile for other titles and home remodeling information go to www.topdrawer.cc.

Made in the USA
Lexington, KY
29 March 2019